This book is a
gift in honor of

_____, an
extraordinary mom.

With love

From_____

Date_____

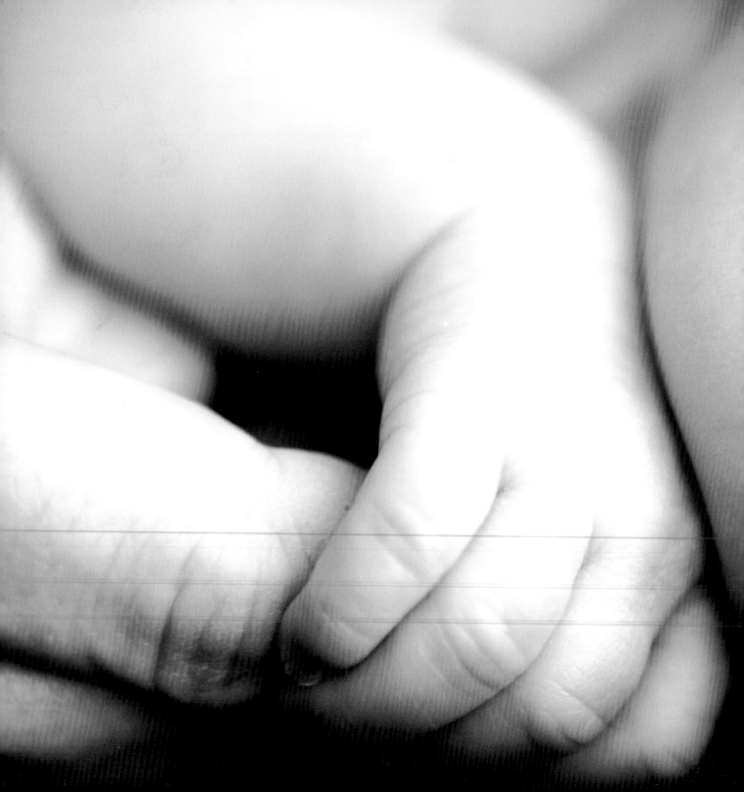

The Greatest Love

The Greatest Love

Being
An Extraordinary
Mom

Loren Slocum

Photography and Design by
BLR Photography

BEFORE YOU WERE CONCEIVED

I WANTED YOU

BEFORE YOU WERE BORN

I LOVED YOU

BEFORE YOU WERE AN HOUR OLD

I WOULD DIE FOR YOU

THIS IS THE MIRACLE OF LOVE.

--Maureen Hawkins

Acknowledgements

This book is dedicated to all those who have reminded me that I am extremely blessed.

My parents, Arlene and Joseph Schandler, who have always instilled in me the knowledge that anything is possible with the power of love and sincere intent. For always cheering me on, even though they sometimes didn't know what they were cheering for. My mother, a woman full of life who makes every moment an adventure, for giving me the insight to trust my creative spirit. My father, for being a living example of God in my life and in the lives of those who have had the good fortune to cross his path. For being the kindest, most patient, and most sincere man I have ever met. You are truly missed but as Quinn said, "they need Papa Dody as an optometrist in heaven."

Shore, for being my number one raving fan, my husband and my best friend. For his reservoir of creativity. For truly believing in my vision, my unique talents, and most of all for believing in the essence of who I am. Finally, for being patient with me and seeking to understand the way I am feeling.

My sons, Josua & Quinn and my daughter Asher, for reminding me what life is about. For being my greatest teachers and a pure examples of unconditional love. For bringing more joy, laughter, and love into my life than I ever thought possible.

My brother, David, for being a constant and solid foundation in my family, whom I feel so lucky to have as my big brother.

God, for blessing me with the gift of motherhood and a chance to play and learn from all the experiences in this life. For the little voice I call intuition which–when I listen to it–always leads me in the right directions.

The BLR Photography team for having such a gifted eye that captures the essence of what this book is about.

Tina Musial, Shannon McCann and Paige Nussbaumer, for seeming to know what I am saying, even when I'm not talking.

Laura Yorke, Editor at Large of Golden Books, for being a walking example of "An Extraordinary Mother." For her creativity and dedication to this book.

Laura Asher, associate editor at St. Martin's, for her love, commitment, and passion for this book.

Jan Miller and her staff at Dupree Miller, for guiding me on the path to make this dream a reality.

The family that I was fortunate enough to become a part of: Heidi, Nancie, Barc (you are missed), TD, Clay, Wendy, Katie, Ova , Earle and in memory of R.C., for making me feel so welcome, loved, and supported by all of you. All my nieces and nephews: Lila, Trinity, Haven, Michael and Caroline.

Heidi Krupp, my one of a kind friend, a woman full of laughter, spirit, and tenacious energy who never takes no for an answer, for her unique ability to always make me feel special. Darren, for being her man!

Mrs. Ross, my fifth grade English teacher, and Herb the Verb!

"My Girls" Onisha, Shareena, Sawkia, Comara, and Juanita, for being my inspirations that lit the candle of desire for me to be a mother. For all of the magic moments we shared together. Now, that you are all grown, may you continue to share your gifts.

My chosen family, who are not blood family but whom I consider as real as any family I have. For challenging me to be my best, and giving me a place to escape the craziness of the world. They are my mentors, sounding boards, guidance counselors, and much more. In one thing I am certain: that whatever I need I can always find within these hearts, minds, and souls...Joelle, Tani, Jayne, Tina, Emily, Cara, Wendy L., Wendy D., Kathy B., Michelle R., Stephanie F., Gina, Alison C., Alissa, Sissy, Linda E., Taylor, Maja, Courtney, Melissa, Melody, Amber, Monique, Anne S., Julie B., Tanya T, Jenn S., Mary G, Pam G, Our Fiji Family, Vanessa, Yehuda, Michal, Esther and the Kabbalah Center. Eric (we miss you so much), Brett, Alphonso, ,Jason, Sam, Rick, Dusty, Matt, Sam, Shaun, Jerome, Tad, Dallyce and Scott.
Cindy, Brenda, Karla and your angel, Ryan, Monty, Adam, Jugat, Satkar. All our friends amazing children: Jackson, Jaxson, Adian, Libby, Joe, Sadie, Maggie, Sammy, Molly, Grace, Collin, Cole, Sienna, Siara, Benny, Ella, Ava, Jag, Kanani and Billie.

And more friends that I don't get to keep in touch with as much but mean so much to me: Joseph and Tina, Deb, Alice, Chris, Maya, Stan, Mandy, Jack, Gary, Pam, John, Jill Rachel, Brannon, Deb C., Joe, William, Vicki, , Ann M., Liz, Sue, and the entire Crew, Trainer teams of the Anthony Robbins Companies Events and every participant I have had the Privilege of teaching at a Life Mastery or Digital Delivery Event.

My mentors: Mother Theresa, every day moms and dads, my parents, Bob Proctor, Wayne Dyer, Mary Manin Morressy, Oprah Winfrey, Rav and Karen Berg, Anthony Robbins.

I have extracted my question process from the work of a good friend–a man I am indebted to, who has dramatically changed the lives of many people around the world Anthony Robbins and his wife Sage.

Each of you will always be a part of me.

I NEVER THOUGHT THAT
YOU SHOULD BE REWARDED FOR
THE GREATEST PRIVILEGE OF LIFE.

-Mary Roper Coker,
on being chosen Mother of the Year 1958

Contents

Forward: A Love Like No Other   xvii
Dear Reader   xxi
Introduction   xxiii

EVERY DAY IS MOTHER'S DAY

Make Every Day Mother's Day   1
Be an Extraordinary Mom   4
Be Yourself   9
Be Wise   13
Be Understanding   17

REFLECTIONS... AN ESSENTIAL TOOL FOR MOTHERHOOD   21

Ask Quality Questions   24
Mommy Morning Questions   31
Mommy Evening Questions   35
Mommy Problem-Solving Questions   39

The Greatest Love MEANS...   47

Truly Loving My Child   49
Being Curious with My Child   53
Being Present with My Child   57
Playing with My Child   61
Showing My Child What Is Possible   65
Teaching and Learning with My Child   69
Having Gratitude and Faith   73

START TODAY   79

A Love Like No Other

For more than twenty years, I have had the extraordinary privilege of being a personal coach to millions of people all over the world and from all walks of life.

My focus has always been to truly serve people by getting them in touch with their own unique gifts–to assist them in appreciating and utilizing their innate capacity to give, grow, learn, love, contribute, and become more that they are presently.

As the parent of four amazing young souls, I know there is nothing more important, challenging, or fulfilling than the love we have for our children. Parenting provides the ultimate challenge and the ultimate gift. It provides us with the leverage to make the most of ourselves, so we have more to give our children. Through parenting, we become teachers, protectors, providers, cheerleaders, disciplinarians, role models, and often, students. By becoming the most outstanding parents we can possibly be, we can raise children to be gifts–gifts we give back to the Creator who gave us life and the world that shaped that life.

That's why I am so excited to introduce you to this book and to its extraordinary author, Loren Slocum. I have known Loren for many years now, and I can tell you that she is an extremely loving person whose commitment to growing and contributing is virtually unmatched.

Loren is not only an extraordinary mom and working mother, but a woman whose commitment to be her best propels her to new heights of joy and passion in both her family life and her business relationships.

This commitment has provided Loren with the drive to create books to help other mothers take their own first steps toward the success and happiness she is experiencing.

It is a privilege to write this foreword for such a dear friend. Loren's heart flows through this book, and the advice she offers may well help you to become the most outstanding mother you can be. Enjoy. And remember, live-and parent-with passion.

-Anthony Robbins

A WOMAN IS THE FULL CIRCLE, WITHIN HER IS THE POWER TO CREATE, NURTURE, AND TRANSFORM.

-Diane Mariechild

$\mathcal{B}$IRTH, n. 1. *The gift of creation.* 2 *The ultimate reflections of God's creative power.* 3. *The beginning of a magical journey.*

Do you remember as a child, when you were given an incredible art assignment or a science fair project to complete? You loved the topic and immediately had all of these great and colorful ideas brewing in your head. Your mind was bursting with the visions of how you thought it would look and feel in the end, even though you hadn't created anything like it before. The images in your head were so vibrant, so alive, you couldn't wait to get started with the process. You knew the finished project would be wonderful, and you threw all of your heart and soul into creating it.

Giving birth also takes your whole heart and soul. You spend your pregnancy with this awesome vision in your head of what your baby may look like and what the baby's personality will be like. You know there is a lot of hard work to be done before you're finished, but you focus all of your concentration and efforts in to making a spectacular creation. You can feel your baby's greatness with every ounce of your being and anticipate the birth with excitement, even though you may have never experienced it before. When you finally get the chance to give birth and see your little miracle, you realize the gift that birth truly is.

Dear Reader,

This book is intended to celebrate you, your child, and the choice you have made to become an extraordinary mother. While each mother has the chance to help her child grow and learn, you have the chance to help your child find their place in the world, now and for the rest of their lives. My highest hope is that by virtue of being a woman and a mother, you acknowledge what a wonderful example you have set for all your loved ones, but most importantly for your child. Within you is the capacity to love more completely than you might think. Within you is the ability to demonstrate to your child the endlessness of your devotion and your commitment to their happiness.

I invite you to make this book your own by placing a favorite picture of you and your precious child here. Choose a photo that reflects a magical moment or special memory that you will keep in your heart forever. Look back on it often to remind yourself what an amazing gift that motherhood is. Gifts are interesting parts of our lives. They are not always neatly wrapped and addressed to use after being on a list we gave to someone else. Gifts like strength, peace and knowledge do not fit into brightly colored boxes with bows. But if there was a time to rip off the wrapping paper to see exactly what YOUR gifts are-now is that time. May this book always remind you of the true unconditional love and wonder that surrounds motherhood. Stay true to who you are.

Loren

*M*AKING
THE DECISION
TO HAVE A CHILD
IS MOMENTOUS.
IT IS TO DECIDE
FOREVER TO HAVE
YOUR HEART GO
WALKING AROUND
OUTSIDE YOUR
BODY.

-Elizabeth Stone

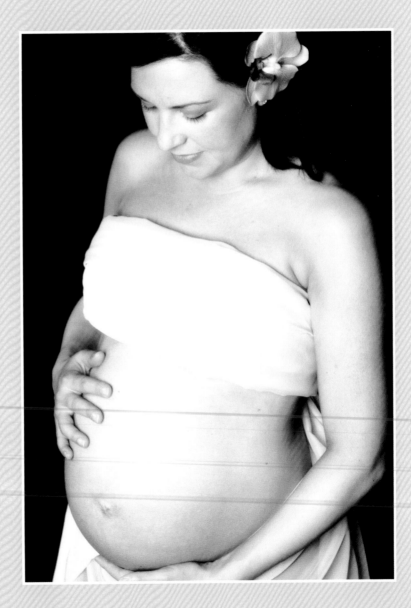

Introduction

It is amazing to me that almost a decade has gone by since I first wrote this book! This book is more than just words. It came from my heart and a culmination of the most exhilarating, mind-bending, and profound journey I ever could have traveled. When I first learned I was pregnant, I was wholly committed to my career, my family, my friends and a litany of community activities and worried about how I would possibly manage the fine act of balancing everything to balance everything. It took a lot of in-depth soul-searching, a little good old-fashioned trial and error, and even a few tears, before I finally came to the realization that I didn't have to sacrifice anything to achieve the balance; I merely had to change my perspective and transform some of the beliefs that were keeping me from reaching my full potential. I had to develop a new attitude – improvise, not compromise.

When talking about all that I have learned since then and the birth of my first son, Josua, everyone kept saying, "Oh, you should update your book because there are so many things that we learn as our children get older. And Quinn, (my youngest son), taught you so many lessons because he was so different than Josua when he was younger!"

Jos was, as everyone would describe, "the perfect baby." He would nurse and then go right to sleep, up for a bit, nurse, and then go right to sleep and that was great. When Quinn came along 4 years later, I thought, "Oh, I totally know what works, what parenting tools I have in my tool belt." Well, well, well, I must say God had other plans for us this time… I broke my foot when I was 7 1/2 months pregnant and was in a cast up until 4 days before he was born. Quinn worked hard to come into this world and his first year was well, shall I say, a learning lesson, for which I am grateful beyond words.

I decided my friends and family might be right and started revising, but noticed as I reread the book and marked the pages needing an update that honestly, not a lot has changed as to the advice I would give. The advice still holds true for not only new parents, but also parents of all ages. The principles in the book remain the same, but how one chooses to implement them at each stage is what will change.

I promise you, when you follow these principles and focus on connecting with your child vs. always seeing how to correct your child, the adventure will be magical. I know, because it worked for me, with Jos as a "perfect baby" and when I kept it simple and listened to Quinn's needs. We developed a strong relationship that continues today. I now am once again following my heart and connecting with my new baby girl in ways that I never imagined I would and have seen the value in discovering the newness of another opportunity to grow as a family.

I couldn't ask for a more magical journey and I wish the same for you. Remember to take the time to truly appreciate the amazing journey you are beginning. It is a huge responsibility, being a mom, but make sure to enjoy the ride, because if they see you are enjoying the ride, they will too!

One in every three kids born in 2000 and beyond will have Type 2 diabetes. That's a shocking statistic, and it's not meant to scare you so much as to make you aware that, just as whatever you put in your own body went into the body you carried inside you, once the baby's born, your healthy (and unhealthy) habits still directly affect your child.

The best thing you can do for your child is to commit to being healthy not just now, while you carry the baby, but for the rest of your life and your child's life. You must create a strong foundation for yourself, so that your children can learn from your example.

Being a mom and being a woman is all part of the whole of who you are now. Everything – positive and negative – that you experience with your child will run over into other areas of your life. If you stress with your kids, stress will be a pattern in the rest of your life. If you live in joy, joy will be the pattern your life takes.

So start today to create healthy habits. Your kids will observe you all the time, seeing how active you are and what you're eating. This need to model healthy habits doesn't stop with the physical, either. You must strive to be healthy in your thoughts and beliefs as well, nurturing your own mind and spirit as well as your body for your own health and the health of your child.

My sons sing this little song: "I love myself so much. So I can love you so much. So you can love you so much. So you can start loving me." You simply can't give what you don't have, so you must acknowledge and love yourself every day.

So many people – moms especially – give and give and give, and they end up running on empty. You only cheat yourself when you do this, though. If you feel like you don't matter, what kind of example are you setting for your child? Do you want them to grow up believing that, when they get older, they won't really matter anymore and that everyone else is more important than they are? When they see you happy and healthy, they'll be happy and healthy.

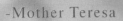

WE DO NO GREAT THINGS, ONLY SMALL THINGS
WITH GREAT LOVE.

-Mother Teresa

EVERY DAY IS MOTHER'S DAY

A mother's incredible love, reassurance, and guidance gives her child the strong foundation needed to confidently face any obstacle that may arise. This foundation provides the safety and support for a child to develop as a strong individual. To celebrate Mother's Day every day, you must celebrate your life and the life you've given to your family, to your community and to the world.

CELEBRATION, n. 1. *An everyday opportunity.*
2. *Gratitude with laughter.* 3. *Dancing to the beat of the heart.*
4. *A party that delights the soul.* 5. *Giving thanks for our blessings.*

A celebration doesn't have to be a perfectly planned and elaborate gala. It can happen over any triumph – whether it is small or large - it can even happen for no reason at all. Think back to what made you celebrate when you were a child. Was it an announcement of an impromptu trip to get ice cream cones with your family? Or maybe you were able to have a carefree day of play with your best friend under a sunny sky. A celebration didn't always have to be a planned party with balloons and cake.

You smiled and laughed aloud while eating your ice cream cone. You twirled in the sunlight and maybe even curled your toes with delight while playing all day. Your inner being was happy and radiant and all seemed good in the world. The smiles and laughter were all a part of your celebration of life. A celebration was and is as much a feeling as it is an act.

Incorporate celebrations in to your life regularly. Look for something small to celebrate when there is no "big" event around the corner. And if there is nothing small to ponder over, create an excuse to celebrate the life you are living.

Make EVERY DAY MOTHER'S DAY

If you believe the greeting card companies and calendar makers, Mother's Day comes just once a year. But we know better! As moms, we know that Mother's Day has little to do with a special mark on a calendar. It's a state of mind–an awareness of the profound role we play in our children's lives each and every day.

Ralph Waldo Emerson once said, "Though we travel the world over to find the beautiful, we must carry it with us or we will find it not." As mothers, we are truly blessed, for we have our children as constant reminders of the beauty of life. With this in mind, our day-to-day activities take on a whole new significance. When you go to the market, you are not just shopping; you are providing nourishment for your loved ones, making simple grocery shopping a much more rewarding experience. When you clean the house, you are creating an environment of peace and order where joy and creativity can flourish unencumbered.

When you run to the department store to purchase clothing for your family, you buy only resilient, quality clothes; it has to protect your family from the elements! When you consistently take care of the necessities of life–your health, finances, career, home, and your own well-being – you are doing so with a greater purpose in mind. You are providing an example of how a person can truly live life with a sense of balance. If you think being a mother is getting your children out of the house by the time they turn eighteen, then you're in for a long, struggle-filled haul! Being an amazing mother every day is an opportunity that has been offered to each of us.

There is a saying–"live each day as if it were your last"–that translates into a belief I hold dear: "Being present in mind, body, and spirit during every precious moment of your life and the lives of others will guarantee a life lived with maximum joy and few regrets."

Each of us is given the same twenty-four hours in a day. How and with whom we decide to spend those hours is totally up to us. As mothers, we make those choices for our children. The daily rituals we establish become the launching pad for the rest of their lives.

At times, we all feel a little off-kilter as mothers. For the most part we learn by watching what others do. We allow what we feel and see to create an "I'm not doing anything right" syndrome because we compare ourselves and our lifestyles to those of other mothers whose lives may not resemble our own at all. We forget that each situation is different and that many choices and different styles of mothering can work. We all should have in common a strong belief that we are amazing moms, in our own right, and do our best to lovingly handle anything that comes our way.

The cause of the "I'm not doing anything right" syndrome may lie in not providing a strong enough foundation for ourselves. Building and strengthening our confidence and self-worth forms a sturdy base from which we can perform consistently and remind ourselves of the most important areas of our life, those priorities that truly shape the emotional foundation of our daily lives.

It is only through our own awakening, our mindful connection with the essence of who we are–givers of life, custodians of the soul–that we can impart true wisdom to our children and make every day a celebration of motherhood.

The cause of the "I'm not doing anything right" syndrome may lie in not providing a strong enough foundation for *ourselves*. Building and strengthening our confidence and self-worth forms a sturdy base from which we can perform consistently and remind ourselves of the most important areas of our life, those priorities that truly shape the emotional foundation of our daily lives.

It is only through our own awakening, our mindful connection with the essence of who we are–givers of life, custodians of the soul–that we can impart true wisdom to our children and make every day a celebration of motherhood.

Be AN EXTRAORDINARY MOM

Being an extraordinary mother is not about going through the daily motions – feeding, bathing, changing, dressing – it's about having a true and loving connection between you and your child everyday; it's about being a steward of your child's joyful development. It's also about making and taking the time to connect with them, discovering the essence of their person, and recognizing their uniqueness. The role of mother goes well beyond correcting your child, making sure their shoelaces are tied and their lunch is packed. Being an extraordinary mom is not what you do; it's about who you are and how you handle things in your life and theirs that make you extraordinary.

You are already extraordinary-did you realize that? By the very act of chosing to become a mom right now, right at this time of your life, you have shown how extraordinary you are!

Choosing to fill your life up with more love for someone new is something that is utterly selfless and absolutely above and beyond anything that could be considered ordinary. You have given a new life a chance to become something brilliant-just by the very fact that you are committing yourself to loving and to nurturing this new piece of your heart.

In choosing to bring this new person into your world, you are showing that you have the capacity to love and to love even more deeply than you ever thought possible.

Imagine your child as the adult you would like him or her to become – happy, loving, conscious, kind, intelligent, patient, giving, strong, and wise. Imagine the kind of mother who would raise a child of that caliber. Now is the time to takes those steps to be that mother…

EVERY CHILD IS OUR OPPORTUNITY TO SHAPE THE FUTURE OF THE WORLD.

-Loren Slocum

*M*OTHERHOOD, n. 1. *The origin of life.* 2. *The shepherding of hope,* 3. *The teaching of love.* 4. *An example of selflessness.* 5. *A chance to positively change the world.*

Do you remember the first time you received a doll? She had long hair, beautiful eyes and her dress was pristine. Immediately, your little heart was in love with this doll, and you cared for her and protected her from everything. You spent hours upon hours dressing her, feeding her, talking to her and letting her take a nap. How many times did you wish she were a real baby, one you could love and care for with all of your heart?

The role of motherhood is cultivated long before any female ever gives birth. Sometimes, even before they can speak, girls are taught to hold and cradle "baby" dolls. Motherhood is such an important and all consuming sought after occupation, that as toddlers and pre-schoolers, girls begin practicing feeding, dressing, and talking with their dolls. The nurturing streak is so strong, it can carry over to include rocks, bugs, sticks and other toys that appear as needing mothering.

Whether this is the first time or your fifth time, becoming a mother is still an exciting time.

Even though dressing and feeding are the day-to-day motions, it sets the stage for how one will interact with their baby in the future. When we played dolls it was important, but we played with our dolls according to what we saw. Whether it was our own mother, a grandmother or relative, we put in to practice the "how" of what we viewed with our dolls. It wasn't what our mothers did, but how they did it that we mimicked.

TO BE A PERSON YOU'RE NOT IS TO WASTE THE PERSON YOU ARE.

-Anonymous

 YOURSELF

We welcome the birth of our children with great celebration, and with good reason! But equally deserving of celebration is the birth of our own motherhood. With this new chapter of life comes the acknowledgment of the unconditional love and support we will provide for our child the minute we find out another person is going to become a part of our lives either through pregnancy or adoption.

You often hear people say, "They broke the mold when she was born." Well, guess what? They did! You are a unique woman and a special mother in many ways. As one of my dear friends always says, "God bless you for being you!" Celebrate you!

Just be yourself. It is obvious to everyone–yourself, your child, and others – when you are being your true self and just as obvious when you are faking it or acting like someone you're not.

Being yourself doesn't mean you shouldn't strive to be better, nor should you stop learning or asking for help. Being yourself means that when you get advice or learn something new, you integrate the parts of what you learned into what already works for your and add your own flair to it.

During your parenting journey, you're going to hear all sorts of advice. Remember, there is more than on way to parent (thankfully!). So develop your own style. Take the best of who you are and let that be the foundation of your parenting style.

Don't change who you are. Continue to be you and all the other "skills" will fall into place. As your child grows, you will grow too. That is the beauty of motherhood... and of life.

 WISE

Wisdom comes from within; looking internally is the best way to solve external challenges. We all possess, deep within ourselves, the knowledge and wisdom to do what is right. God only gives us the challenges he knows we can handle. We intuitively know the correct path to take if we just pause a moment in our hurried lives to focus our minds and trust the answers that come to us. The people to admire most are those who take a deep breath before they make a decision, who use calm conviction to move forward with love and compassion, rather that those who get swallowed up by the emotion of the moment. Adopting a calm, determined, and sometimes daring approach to life is an excellent lesson for your children and possibly the wisest step you will ever take for yourself.

As mothers, we must trust the wisdom with which God has blessed us in order to make decisions for ourselves and our children–decisions that feel right. Remember, the decisions you make may not always achieve your desired result, but no decision is wrong if you choose to learn something from it. What an extraordinary role model you will be for your child, if you approach life with this type of attitude. Your child will see a mother willing to make mistakes, but not willing to give up!

LET NO MAN BE DELUDED THAT A KNOWLEDGE OF THE PATH CAN SUBSTITUTE FOR PUTTING ONE FOOT IN FRONT OF THE OTHER.

-Mary Caroline Richards

EVERY WOMAN
SHOULD REMEMBER
THAT WE HAVE THE
INTUITIVE RADAR TO
KNOW EXACTLY HOW
TO LISTEN TO OUR
CHILDREN, WHAT TO
SAY TO OUR CHILDREN,
AND HOW TO LOVE
OUR CHILDREN....
WE LEARN WHAT THEY
WANT, WE LEARN
WHAT THEY NEED,
BY LISTENING TO
THEM AND WATCHING
THEM. THEY KNOW, AND
THEY WILL TELL US.

-Marianne Williamson

 UNDERSTANDING

Being understanding means being compassionate, open, intuitive, and present in mind and in body. The first step toward understanding is truly listening–with your heart. Remember, hearing is not the same as listening. You can hear someone's voice, but are you really listening to his or her message?

Can you listen to your child's hopes, dreams and fears? These moments are the times when you can prove yourself as the best mother possible. Listening requires that you still the inside thoughts in your mind and begin to really understand what your child wants you to learn from THEIR experiences.

With the many challenges and activities that life provides us, it can often be easier to react than to try to understand what is going on with our children. When your child is first born, you hone these listening skills; your baby cannot utter a word, yet you innately know when he is hungry, tired, or uncomfortable just by the way he cries or fusses.

Keep these same listening skills with you even when your children can talk; try to understand how they are feeling, not just what they are saying. This level of caring will transform your relationship with your child. It will help you avoid conflict, build trust, and strengthen the special bond between the two of you.

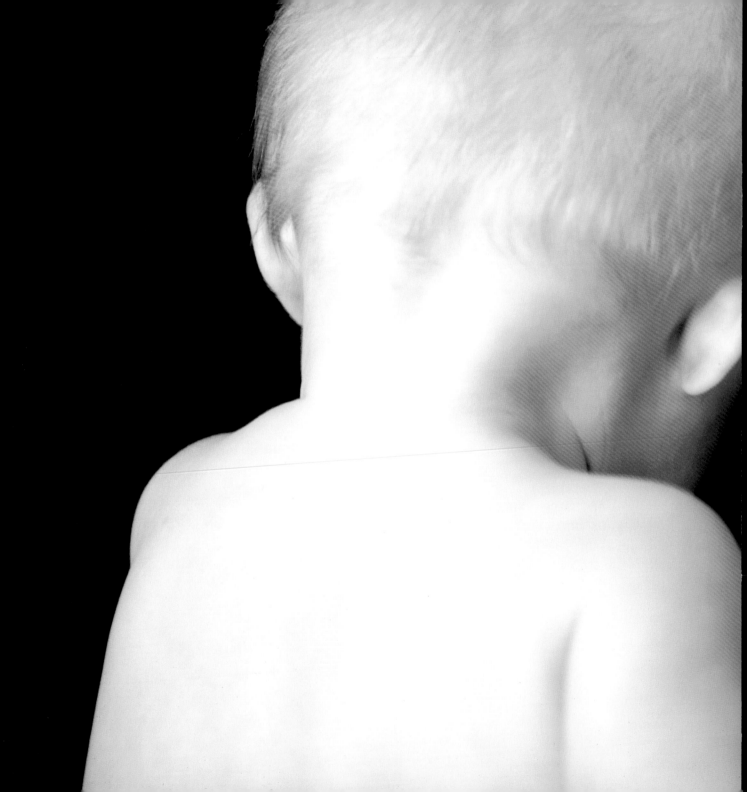

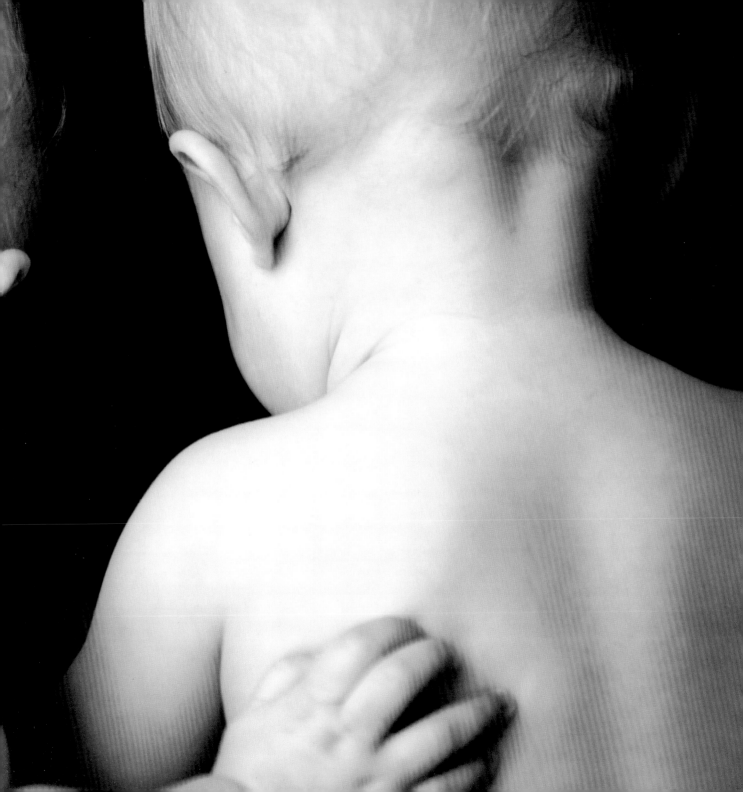

REFLECTIONS...
AN ESSENTIAL TOOL FOR MOTHERHOOD

Ask meaningful questions of yourself in moments of quiet reflection and expect quality answers. Such reflection will take you directly to the heart of the matter, to what is most important for you to learn. Reflection means taking the time to search and discover new ways to improve yourself, your child, and your life as a mother.

You may already have noticed that everyone has an opinion, and everyone's opinion is based on what they believe is most important: your mother and mother-in-law, aunts, friends, husband, his friends and their wives, books and magazine articles, and so forth. You must look inside, listen to your heart, and let it tell you what is right for you.

The PRESENT, n. 1. *The moment when you open your eyes. 2. A timeless second. 3. A state of being in the moment. 4. When you move from your head to your heart. 5. The determination of your future. 6. A precious gift.*

There are moments when all of the pieces of your life come together and fit perfectly. You are utterly content with your surroundings and everything going on in your life for that sliver of time that you want to grasp it, and never let go. You want to always remain in that place, in that second, the present of your life and revel in it. You don't think the future can get any better than what your present is doing that moment.

Those golden moments of our present eventually fade in to the past. When we move forward and carry those memories with us, we have the knowledge that we can achieve more golden moments anytime, anywhere we please, with a little effort. All of our present times can be golden and we should treasure them, just because we are blessed to have them.

Ask Quality Questions

As moms, we have an awesome responsibility and privilege: We truly mold the leaders of the next generation. The first human contact our babies have is with us. Through our touch, they learn love, caring, tenderness, safety, and strength. And as our babies become more fully a part of the world, they learn by observing the example we set. Our actions make a much bigger impression than our words, so we must always act in the best, most positive manner.

The right questions work to focus your intention and your attention to your child.

A valuable tool that allows me to act positively on a daily basis, rather than settle for my second best, is to ask myself quality questions. Specifically, I ask myself the "Mommy Morning Questions," the "Mommy Evening Questions," and the "Mommy Problem-Solving Questions." How powerful are these questions? Quite simply, they can change your life. No matter how heavy the demands on your time and energy, taking a moment or two to reflect on these questions can move you instantly from feeling overwhelmed and exhausted to feeling excited, grateful, passionate, and energized.

We experience everything through our own filters of the world. Something that seems terrible or tragic to one person may be incredible and uplifting to another. These questions are designed to assist you in creating better filters for yourself, so you get more out of each day, each situation, and each precious moment.

You may think you do not have the time to answer such questions, but you must commit to making the time. Just as you make time for other things that are truly important–like feeding your baby, changing your baby's diaper, or giving your baby a bath–above all, you must make time to raise an exceptional child. Quality questions can be a powerful tool to help you do just that. These questions have served as lifesavers for me in all sorts of situations, and I know they can be the same for anyone else who has too much to do and too little time–in short, for anyone who is a mom!

CLEVER PEOPLE SEEM NOT TO FEEL THE
NATURAL PLEASURE OF BEWILDERMENT,
AND ARE ALWAYS ANSWERING QUESTIONS
WHEN THE CHIEF RELISH OF A LIFE
IS TO GO ON ASKING THEM.

-Frank Moore Colby, "Simple Simon," The Colby Essays

KEYS TO ASKING QUESTIONS AND HAVING THEM WORK:

🏵 YOU MUST ASK EACH QUESTION UNTIL YOU COME UP WITH THE ANSWER THAT IS RIGHT FOR YOU. If you ask a question like, "What is my child going to teach me today?" then focus on how this answer can make a positive difference in your child's day and, ultimately, his life.

🏵 YOU MUST TAKE A MOMENT TO SEARCH YOUR HEART FOR EACH ANSWER. Once you come up with the answer that is right for you, take in a deep breath and acknowledge its potential impact. It is way too simple to want to stop at the first question or the answer you think it should be.

❁ ASK THESE QUESTIONS CONSISTENTLY. The more you ask the questions, the better you will be at finding meaningful answers that come from your heart. I ask these questions a minimum of once a day. I come up with answers quickly because I have conditioned myself through repetition. You will find that the answers become more and more profound each day. Also, by making the question-asking process a habit, you will start to notice that you automatically ask them at other times during your day. Many times I have had problems arise; I am immediately able to ask myself a "Mommy Problem-Question," and the answer helps me to transcend that problem.

❁ READ THE QUESTIONS AND GET IN THE HABIT OF USING THEM. Put them on little cards you see every day. Put the "Mommy Morning Questions" on your bathroom mirror, the "Mommy Evening Questions" on your night stand, and the "Mommy Problem-Solving Questions" in your purse. The next time a challenging situation arises and you find yourself getting panicky or "losing it," just stop, take a few deep breaths, start asking yourself these great questions, and focus on all the wonderful answers you devise. I guarantee these question/answer sessions will make a huge difference in the way you react. Why is that important? Because little eyes are always watching.

MOMMY MORNING

QUESTIONS

How can my child and I
experience our love in an
extraordinary new way today?

This set of questions is designed to help you start your day in the best possible emotional place for you and your child, and to assist you in focusing on what will really make a difference in your life and your child's. By asking yourself these questions every morning, you will uncover opportunities for learning, growth, love, patience, happiness, and many other powerful emotions that you might otherwise overlook in your busy daily life.

TEACHING ~ LEARNING

What is my baby going to teach me today?

What am I going to teach my baby today?

What can I do today to help my child learn and grow?

What can I do today to learn and grow?

How can I be a role model for my baby today?

How is my child going to be a role model for me today?

What lessons can I teach my child today?

What will I encourage my child to learn today?

CONNECTION & LOVE

In the midst of my busy day, how can I still remain grateful?

How can I be even more patient today?

Who do I love?

Who loves me?

How can I show my love even more?

What can I do today to feel more connected to my child?

Am I taking the time to present in the moment?

How can I thank others for the love they share with me?

FUN & LAUGHTER

What am I most excited about today?

What am I proudest of in my life today?

What am I most grateful for in my life today?

How can I create even more special moments for my family and myself?

How can I take even better care of my family and myself?

What is something special that I can do for my baby and myself today?

Who is my child going to become because of me today?

OTHER PEOPLE IN MY LIFE HAVE HELPED MY
SOUL TO SING A SONG.... YOU, MY CHILD, HAVE
CAUSED MY HEART TO SING A SYMPHONY.

-DONNA RINGO

MOMMY EVENING QUESTIONS

What did my child and I learn
from each other today?

This set of questions is your greatest teacher. We become better at something by looking at our progress along the way. These questions give you a chance to increase your awareness of how you are connecting with your child: Where are the gaps in your child's growth, in your growth as a family, in your becoming the best mom you can be?

Remind yourself that you will rarely, if ever, be perfect, but the most profound growth will come from your pursuit of being the best mom you can be. The key is to become just a tiny bit better every day. This is where the greatest rewards are hidden.

Self ~ Care

Did I pause and breathe today?

How did I take care of myself physically today?

Did I balance what I needed to do with what I wanted to accomplish today?

Did I eat well today?

How can I care for myself even better tomorrow?

Fun & Laughter

What did my baby do to make me laugh?

What did I do to make my baby laugh?

What was a magic moment from today?

How else can I bring even more fun and laughter into our lives?

CONNECTION & LOVE

What did my baby and I do together today?

How many times did my baby hear me say, "I love you"?

How did I express love and gratitude today? To myself, to my child, to my family?

TEACHING

What did I learn today that will make me a better woman?

How did I see things from my baby's perspective?

How did I help my child interact with the world today?

REFLECTION

What made me smile today?

What made me proud today?

How was I a great mom today?

What was I truly grateful today?

IMPORTANT VERSUS URGENT

What worked today?

Did I focus on what was truly important today?

Was I happy at least 90 percent of the time today?

How could I be even happier tomorrow?

$\mathcal{M}$OMMY
PROBLEM ~ SOLVING
QUESTIONS

What would an extraordinary mom

do in this situation?

As a mother, you will be tested again and again–perhaps more than in any other role you perform in life. There will be tests of patience, love, perseverance, endurance, selflessness, caring, maturity, compassion, and discipline–more tests than you could have ever imagined before you actually became a mom.

How you respond to these tests will provide your moments of greatest growth, learning, and teaching. These questions will offer you a helping hand to face the never-ending challenges of being a busy mom. They will help you to focus on getting through a situation and, more important, on becoming a better mom, strengthening you and, in turn, your child, with the resolution of each situation.

When you feel like you're at your wit's end, take a deep breath and realize that you will make it thorough even the most difficult moments. Even when an experience is painful, it will ultimately make you a better mom, and one day you will realize that it is all worth it.

Really be aware of what is happening with your child. Avoid the temptation to just rely on "Oh, he's two. That's why he's acting this way." Instead, when you realize that something isn't right, ask yourself why your child might be feeling this way. Ask yourself what you can do, what questions you can ask, to try to understand. How can you try to help your child feel better? How can you help him or her to be stronger and healthier?

The answers that come to you will be your answers and therefore what's right for you and your child. If you feel you'd like others' input, ask a couple of people you trust what they would do in your situation. Of their responses, what makes the most sense to you? Don't over think the situation; get out of your head and really listen to your heart. Do your best to avoid creating complications where there are none.

What would an extraordinary mom do in this situation?

How am I going to grow as a result of this challenge?

How will this moment serve me, my baby, and my family?

How is my baby going to become a better adult because of the way I handle this experience?

How can I find more patience, love, strength, or resourcefulness right now?

IF A CHILD IS TO KEEP ALIVE HIS INBORN SENSE OF WONDER, HE NEEDS THE COMPANIONSHIP OF AT LEAST ONE ADULT WHO CAN SHARE IT, REDISCOVERING WITH HIM THE JOY, EXCITEMENT, AND MYSTERY OF THE WORLD WE LIVE IN.

-Rachel Carson, The Sense of Wonder

CHILD, n. 1. A gift from God to be handled with care. 2. An open path of love. 3. True innocence. 4. Hope for a better world.

Imagine the delicate petals on a flower, the bright red of an apple from a tree or the graceful wings on a butterfly. You can see their beauty by looking, but you want to delve in and experience it with more of your senses. You try a smell, a touch or even a taste of the creation before you, eager to experience all of it. Once you have a deeper understanding of how it was created, you recognize its innocence and purity. You want to maintain that purity, and do everything in your power to protect and preserve the innocence.

A child will also elicit those emotions from you. You see their outward beauty first, but then are mesmerized by their trusting actions, naïve words and deeds, and want to keep them forever innocent. You will do everything in your power to protect the child as it matures and follows the path you set in place as a mother.

In a very real sense, you have been reborn as well when you have a child. Though you have a wealth of experience and knowledge from the years of your life, your child will create a whole new world, a new landscape for you.

Few people get the chance to truly rediscover their own lives, so it makes sense that you should cherish this time as something uniquely special.

A child is your hope for something better in this world-and not just for the benefit of others, but also for the benefit of yourself and your ability to hold that hope for the world.

The Greatest *love* means...

TO LOVE AND TO BE LOVED IS
TO FEEL THE SUN FROM BOTH SIDES.

--David Viscott

TRULY LOVING A CHILD

Truly loving my little one means making sure that he has all the things he needs, not just the basics of clothing, food, shelter and warmth, but also the intangibles like values, morals, confidence, standards, and, most important, love.

Love is the foundation for creating anything of meaning in life, especially when raising a child. Working from a strong foundation of love, all things seem possible because we feel a sense of glorious abundance flowing through us. We seem to have more to give than we ever thought possible. A love so full and so complete creates a unique bond between mother and child—a love that only grows stronger with each new experience.

You will be truly startled and overjoyed to see just how many new experiences are waiting to happen all in the eyes and the heart of your child.

Cherish this level of love and take the time to communicate that affection to your child through your touch, your patience, your understanding, and your actions. This level of intimacy will allow you and your baby to appreciate and experience the world more profoundly.

Loving Mom

Mom always takes time to show me and tell me she loves me. I can see Mom's love for me in her eyes. I can feel her love in every little touch. I can hear the love in her beautiful voice. I have the most loving mom in the world!

ℬEING CURIOUS WITH MY CHILD

Children look at the world in the most innocent and curious way—their eyes full of wonder and awe. Having a child offers us the opportunity to rediscover the wonders of the world. If you are looking for a new perspective on life, kneel down beside your baby and take a look at the world from her vantage point. Go ahead... get down on the floor and try to comprehend the thoughts that must be racing through your baby's mind as she delicately twists each fiber of your plush carpeting or tries to nibble her own little toes. There are so many ways to encourage your baby to make new discoveries. Exploring the world, hand in hand, makes life a bright package just waiting to be opened.

Adventure Mom

My mom is always showing me that life is an adventure. Looking at each and every experience as a chance to discover—discover the unknown, discover the possibilities. Sometimes, adventures can be scary, like learning to walk, falling off my bed, or learning to ice skate, but my mom makes sure I celebrate each of these opportunities She reminds me that these experiences help me to joyfully anticipate future adventures—some I will share with her and some I will discover on my own.

Start TODAY AS A CHILD DOES, FULL OF LIGHT
AND THE CLEAREST VISION.

--Brenda Veland

$\mathcal{B}$EING PRESENT WITH MY CHILD

When you're feeding, bathing, and playing with your baby, are you giving him your full attention? Your undivided attention means "being present" with your child. Each moment you spend together is a gift that allows you to connect more intimately with your little one.

The first key to being present is to listen, not just with your ears, but with your heart. Look for the real meaning in your baby's communication. By learning to understand your child's subtle messages you will strengthen the tremendous bond between the two of you.

The second key to being present is to see, not only with your eyes, but with your soul. A mother's intuition is often a clearer window to her child's soul than the naked eye. Choose to be present with your baby in mind, body, and spirit—giving your whole self in each moment you spend with your little angel will add incredible joy and fulfillment to motherhood.

If you can't be physically present as much as you might like, you can't feel guilty about that. Think of your situation in terms of intention: If you have the intention to take care of your child, and you have to work, you're not being a bad mom, you're providing for your child. Because your intention is a good one, working is the right thing to do. Rather than feeling guilty about working, commit when you get home to really being present with your child.

Cuddle, read, talk, or do whatever makes you both feel good when you're together. Being present with your child will make a major difference in your life. Everything that builds a better relationship with your child will also apply to your relationships with your friends, spouses, and significant others. When you make being fully present with your children a priority, it becomes your way of being all the time, in all circumstances. So you will not only be a better mom, but also a better partner and a better friend.

Playful Mom

My mom and I play in lots of different ways. Sometimes, my mom shares her special treasures with me. Mommy loves watching me discover the beauty of the simplest gifts that some grown-ups take for granted. What means the most to me is when my mommy says I remind her to stop and celebrate life every chance she can! I'm happy when everything my mom does is play to her!

PLAYING WITH MY CHILD

How lucky you are! You finally have a perfectly adorable little excuse to be a kid again (no matter what your driver's license may say)—to play silly games and make funny faces, to build sand castles on the beach, to swing on the swing set, and to test out all the possible toys your child might desire. Playing with your child may just be the easiest part of motherhood, or at least the most fun. So what does it truly entail? Time—a hot commodity in today's hustle-bustle world—and imagination. Be creative and be generous, because time spent playing with your child is the most precious time of all—for both of you.

Who can make the funniest face?

How many tickle spots can you find?

Who can hop like a bunny rabbit? "Ribbit" like a frog?

What amazing adventure will the two of you take?
(A trip to the store or reading a story).

What can you create today?

What funny noises can you make?

JUST PLAY

Present Mom

When my mommy and I are together, she gives me her full attention. S
understands what I need and want even though I can't talk as well as
she can. The biggest gift my mommy gives me is just spending time w
me. She is definitely a "present" mom!

SHOWING MY CHILD WHAT IS POSSIBLE

How many times do we impose limits on those we love without ever realizing what we are doing? The purpose of the fences we put up is, more often than not, to keep those we care about from getting hurt.

It is our job to protect our children and to make sure they follow the "right path."

Finding the "right path" is a difficult task—a path that leads one child to the promised land may lead another child astray. Let your children take risks. Let them find their calling. Let them experience what their hearts tell them to experience.

One of the best ways you can help them find their paths is by following you own calling, fulfilling your special purpose on this earth. You can also expose your child to as many different experiences as you can. Take them to places you love, and to places you wouldn't go to on your own in a million years—an art museum or a war memorial, a ceramics class or a woodworking shop, the beach or the mountains. Go to a classical music concert. Eat at a Greek tavern. Your children will know what lies ahead in this great big world if you take the time to show them all the wonderful gifts available.

You know what else might happen? You might enjoy all the new experiences yourself! Remember, don't "freak out" if your child tries something and fails or doesn't enjoy it. To teach your children what is possible, you must allow them to fail and, more important, to succeed through their own discoveries. With supervised self-discovery, you will help them learn and grow as individuals.

Who knows? You might change your mind about what is possible too!

Example Mom

Mom never lets other people's limits stop her from being the best in the whole wide world. My mom shows me what is good and honest and true not only by telling me but by showing me with her actions. She is truly an example of what is possible if you really believe.

When I grow up, I want to be just like her.

TEACHING AND LEARNING WITH MY CHILD

Life offers so much to learn and experience that it can be hard to know where to begin. Even as you lead the way, your child teaches you in turn. Through our children, we see the world with new vision, hear life in different harmonies, and feel textures through the hands of a fresh new soul.

Just when you think you are done learning, your child will show you more. This is the time to be open to this experience and to the newness behind every smile, behind every whisper that only you can hear.

This new reaction to the world is an important reminder that one of the primary roles of motherhood is to teach. During your teaching, you will often find the roles reversed, as though God sent your child to you to be your teacher. At different moments, you will sit in awe as your child discovers something so simple yet so new—and through her wonder, you will be transformed.

Learning will come in ways you never imagined or planned. Sometimes the lessons shared by you and your child will come in your wildest moments together. You cannot plan everything you want to occur in order to teach your child the lessons of life. My son's godmother once said, "If you want to make God laugh, tell him your plan." In other words, for all the things you want to teach your child, there will be an equal number for you to learn. Be grateful for the opportunity to learn from the honest innocence of your child's soul.

Teacher Mom

Mom always wants me to find the best, deep inside myself. She helps me to walk, talk, learn, and laugh. She shows me new things like animals, sand castles, puddles, and rainbows and explains them to me. She always looks for the good I have inside me and then helps me express it to the world.

LORD OF THE
LOVING HEART,
MAY MINE BE
LOVING TOO.
LORD OF THE
GENTLE HANDS,
MAY MINE BE
GENTLE TOO.
LORD OF THE
WILLING FEET,
MAY MINE BE
WILLING TOO.
SO I MAY GROW
MORE LIKE THEE
IN ALL I SAY AND DO.

--Phyllis Garlick

Having Gratitude and Faith

Give thanks that you have been blessed with a wonderful baby. Motherhood is an unparalleled privilege. Your duty is to love your baby no matter who or what he or she becomes. Never compare your baby to others. Your baby may have physical or mental limitations, but you must believe that those extra challenges were given to your family for a reason. Believe that God thought you were one of the few people who could handle such a challenge, and that is why you were given such a special child.

I believe that God chooses your baby and your baby's personality to help you become the best person you can possibly be. Have faith that you will be guided to make the choices that allow you and your child to grow. With both of my boys and my daughter, I am so grateful that I have taken the time to really connect with them, whether I was feeding them, playing with them, teaching them something new or just taking the time to stare into their beautiful faces. I have never taken a second of that time for granted. I have really cherished each moment, realizing that they'll only be little for so long.

What I've really learned is not to take anything for granted as if it will always be there for me. Never lose your sense of wonder and blessing at having a child. Always be grateful. And let your gratitude extend beyond your life as a mother. I'm more grateful for everything now and more aware.

Being a mother is an honor and a challenge; we mold a tiny fragment of the future in our hands. I hope you, too, have these incomparable feelings. As mothers, if we commit to raising better children, I honestly believe we can heal the world one soul at a time.

Angel Mom

To me, my mom is an angel. She is so pure and so special.
Her eyes reach souls. Her touch mends hearts. She is sweet yet
strong, simple yet elegant. Sometimes, if I really concentrate, I
can see the glow of the halo above her head. My mom is truly
the loveliest woman you will ever behold.

You MUST BE THE CHANGE YOU WISH
TO SEE IN THE WORLD.

--Gandhi

Start Today

We as mothers have been entrusted to provide a physical and emotional environment that nurtures, teaches, and inspires our children. At the beginning of a new millennium, a time of unforeseen challenge and opportunity, we must rise to our gift of being mothers.

Commit to a life that continues to make love the number one priority and a life where you truly cherish each moment. Enjoy the journey.

Know that you're an extraordinary woman who has been blessed with an amazing opportunity: to change the world through your children. The decisions we make with our children will truly shape the future of the world. If we teach them to be kind, the world will be kind. If we teach them to ignore each other, they'll ignore each other. If we teach them to live in fear, they'll live in fear. If we teach them to love no matter what, they'll love no matter what.

There is truly no time like the present and all of its ability to gift us with knowledge, guidance, hope and so much more.

$\mathcal{A}$ BABY IS GOD'S OPINION...
THAT THE WORLD SHOULD GO ON.

--Carl Sandburg

THE FUTURE, n, 1. A reward for being active in the present. 2. A place of curiosity. 3. Fast paced. 4. Your choice!

Do you remember working so hard to keep the leaves out of an elderly neighbor's yard one fall? Or did you help shovel snow with your parents all winter long just because? Your heart grew warm from the thanks and gratitude you received, while knowing you made a small difference in someone's life. However, you didn't know those moments would be a key part to your developing future. Your hard work in the neighborhood was rewarded with a scholarship and community recognition. You continued to give back to the neighborhood to repay the recognition, but you earned more recognition, which helped you land a job, find a new house or even make a new friend.

The actions we take now as mothers help to shape the futures of our children. Much like the bulb or the seed we plant into the ground now, our actions may not seem to be taking root, but once they are ready to bloom, we can smile and recognize the part we had played in the process.

The future is yet to be determined by our actions of today. The actions you take now while traveling along the motherhood journey can and will shape the future. If we do not take any actions today, there may not be the blossoming flower in the years to come. While it is true there will be times when things are difficult, and times when we feel like nothing we do is ever right for our child, in our hearts we know that our love is going to enrich our child.

Use every opportunity available which the present offers to shape your future and the future of your child. Be the active mom that wants to learn about their child's dreams. Ask questions and be involved in things they do.

Instead of simply hoping for the best, we can take action NOW, RIGHT NOW, to help craft a future that is not only blooming for our children, but also for ourselves.

This is a test of you and your desire to give of yourself, your love and your gentle strength to this amazing child. You will succeed in your special way. It may not look like how your friend parents or your parents did but just know you will succeed and you have all of the resources to do exactly that.

Enjoy this journey!

ABOUT THE AUTHOR

Many who have attended events with Loren call her "The Real Deal". She is a wife, mother, author, businesswoman and active volunteer for many organizations. Loren Slocum's The Greatest Love illustrates her passion for life, as witnessed by thousands of women and men throughout the world. This passion keeps her vibrant and young, and magnifies her extraordinary relationship with her family and her career.

As Founder, CEO and President of Lobella International, Loren has inspired thousands of women to stay true to who they are. She is committed to helping women realize their natural gifts and talents. Loren is also the co-founder of Project Boomerang, in addition to being an International speaker, coach and certified nutritional therapist. She lives with her husband Shore, in Nevada with three of their greatest accomplishments, Josua, Quinn and Asher.

For more information on Loren Slocum's upcoming events, attending one of her seminars or getting the The Greatest Love CD or any of her other products visit www.lorenslocum.com and lobella.com. 10% of all book sales ordered off Lobella.com will be donated to Women and Children's Organizations.

ABOUT THE PHOTOGRAPHER

Brittany Hanson is known as a powerful and passionate photographer. Having photographed some of the world's most prominent families, their babies, as well as their weddings, Brittany is an example of truly loving what you do.

A native of Las Vegas, where she resides now with her husband, Eric (her high school sweetheart) and their children Kai and Dylan. Brittany's images of life, love and laughter began to surface out into the public shortly after the birth of her first child. She found instant inspiration in becoming a mother and found her biggest passion – photographing life itself. Her diverse images have one thing in common, that they are real, and that you can experience a little bit of each person's soul from them. Brittany's published work ranges from the web, magazine covers, advertising, and awards from within the professional photography industry.

Today this mother of two enjoys a nonstop career traveling worldwide to share her passion in photographing life at its finest moments. For more info regarding Brittany Lee Hanson's work, visit her online portfolio at www.blrphoto.com